9-1 G(
NOT   )
ISHIGURO'S
NEVER LET ME GO
- Study guide (All chapters, page-by-page analysis)

by Joe Broadfoot

The right of Joe Broadfoot to be identified as the author of this work has been asserted in accordance with Section 77 of the Copyright, Designs and Patents Act 1988

**ISBN-13:
978-1537415079**

**ISBN-10:
1537415077**

CONTENTS

9-1 GCSE REVISION NOTES – NEVER LET ME GO

Brief Introduction

This book is aimed at GCSE students of English Literature who are studying Kazuo Ishiguro's *Never Let Me Go*. The focus is on what examiners are looking for, especially since the changes to the curriculum in 2015, and here you will find each chapter covered in detail. I hope this will help you and be a valuable tool in your studies and revision.

Criteria for high marks

Make sure you use appropriate critical language (see glossary of literary terms at the back). You need your argument to be fluent, well-structured and coherent. Stay focused!

Analyse and explore the use of form, structure and the language. Explore how these aspects affect the meaning.

Make connections between texts and look at different interpretations. Explore their strengths and weaknesses. Don't forget to use supporting references to strengthen your argument.

Analyse and explore the context.

Best essay practice

There are so many way to write an essay. Many schools use **PEE** for paragraphs: point/evidence/explain. Others use **PETER**: point/evidence/technique/explain/reader; **PEEL**: point, example, explain, link; **PEEE**: point/evidence/explain/explore. Whichever method you use, make sure you mention the **writer's effects**. This generally is what most students forget to add. You must think of what the writer is trying to achieve by using a particular technique and what is actually achieved. Do not just spot techniques and note them. You may get some credit for using appropriate technology, but unless you can comment on the effect created on the reader and/or the writer's intention, you will miss out on most of the marks available.

Essay planning

In order to write a good essay it is necessary to plan. In fact, it is best to quite formulaic in an exam situation, as you won't have much time to get started. Therefore I will ask you to learn the following acronym: **DATMC (Definition, Application, Terminology, Main, Conclusion**. Some schools call it: **GSLMC (General, Specific, Link, Main, Conclusion)**, but it amounts to the same thing. The first three letters concern the introduction. (Of course, the alternative is to leave some blank lines and write your introduction after you have completed the main body of your essay, but it is probably not advisable for most students).

Let us first look at the following exam question, which is on poetry (of course, the same essay-planning principles apply to essays on novels and plays as well).

QUESTION: Explore how the poet conveys **feelings** in the poem.

STEP ONE: Identify the **keyword** in the question. (I have already done this, by highlighting it in **bold**). If you are following GSLMC, you now need to make a **general statement** about what feelings are. Alternatively, if you're following DATMC, simply **define** 'feelings'. For example, 'Feelings are emotion states or reactions or vague, irrationals ideas and beliefs'.

STEP TWO: If you are following GSLMC, you now need to make a **specific statement** linking feelings (or whatever else you've defined) to how they appear in the poem.

Alternatively, if you're following DATMC, simply define which 'feelings' **apply** in this poem. For example, 'The feelings love, fear and guilt appear in this poem, and are expressed by the speaker in varying degrees.'

STEP THREE: If you are following GSLMC, you now need to make a **link statement** identifying the methods used to convey the feelings (or whatever else you've defined) in the poem. Alternatively, if you're following DATMC, simply define which **techniques** are used to convey 'feelings' in this poem. For example, 'The poet primarily uses alliteration to emphasise his heightened emotional state, while hyperbole and enjambment also help to convey the sense that the speaker is descending into a state of madness.

STEP FOUR: Whether you are following GSLMC or DATMC, the next stage is more or less the same. The main part of the essay involves writing around **six paragraphs**, using whichever variation of PEEE you prefer. In my example, I will use **Point, Evidence, Exploration, Effect** on the listener. To make your essay even stronger, try to use your quotations chronologically. It will be easier for the examiner to follow, which means you are more likely to achieve a higher grade. To be more specific, I recommend that you take and analyse two quotations from the beginning of the poem, two from the middle, and two at the end.

STEP FIVE: Using Carol Ann Duffy's poem, 'Stealing', here's an example of how you could word one of your six paragraphs: **(POINT)** 'Near the beginning of the poem, the speaker's determination is expressed.' **(EVIDENCE)** 'This is achieved through the words: 'Better off dead than giving in'. **(EXPLORATION)**. The use of 'dead' emphasizes how far the speaker is prepared to go in pursuit of what he wants, although there is a sense that he is exaggerating (hyperbole). **(EFFECT)** The listener senses that the speaker may be immature given how prone he is to exaggerate his own bravery.

STEP SIX: After writing five or more paragraphs like the one above, it will be time to write a **conclusion**. In order to do that, it is necessary to sum up your previous points and evaluate them. This is not the time to introduce additional quotations. Here is an example of what I mean: 'To conclude, the poet clearly conveys the speaker's anger. Although the listener will be reluctant to completely sympathise with a thief, there is a sense that the speaker is suffering mentally, which makes him an interesting and partially a sympathetic character. By using a dramatic monologue form, the poet effectively conveys the speaker's mental anguish, which makes it easier to more deeply understand what first appears to be inexplicable acts of violence.

Other tips

Make your studies active!

Don't just sit there reading! Never forget to annotate, annotate and annotate!

All page references refer to the 2006 paperback edition of *Never Let Me Go* published by Faber & Faber Ltd, London (ISBN-13: 978-0-571-25809-3).

Never Let Me Go

AQA (New specification starting in 2015)

If you're studying for an AQA qualification in English Literature, there's a good chance your teachers will choose this text to study. There are good reasons for that: it's moralistic in that the text encourages us to think about right and wrong.

Never Let Me Go is one of the texts listed on Paper 2, which needs to be completed in 2 hours 15 minutes. Your writing on the essay will only be part of the exam, however, and for the rest of time you will need to write about poetry: two poems categorised as 'Unseen Poetry' and two poems from the AQA anthology.

AQA have given students a choice of 12 set texts for the Modern Texts section of the exam paper. There are 6 plays: JB Priestley's *An Inspector Calls*, Willy Russell's *Blood Brothers*, Alan Bennett's *The History Boys*, Dennis Kelly's *DNA*, Simon Stephens's script of *The Curious Incident of the Dog* in the *Night-Time*, and Shelagh Delaney's *A Taste of Honey*. Alternatively, students can chose to write on the following 6 novels: William Golding's *Lord of the Flies*, AQA's Anthology called *Telling Tales*, George Orwell's *Animal Farm*, Kazuo Ishiguro's *Never Let Me Go*, Meera Syal's *Anita and Me*, and Stephen Kelman's *Pigeon English*. Answering one essay question on one of the above is worth a total of 34 marks, which includes 4 for vocabulary, spelling, punctuation and grammar. In other words, this section is worth 21.25% of your total grade at GCSE.

AQA have produced a poetry anthology entitled *Poems, Past and Present,* which includes 30 poems. Rather than study all 30, students are to study one of the two clusters of 15, which concentrate on common themes. There are two themes which students can choose from: Love and relationships, or power and conflict. Within the chosen thematic cluster, students must study all 15 poems and be prepared to write on any of them. Answering this section is worth 18.75% of your total GCSE grade.

The 'unseen poetry' section is more demanding, in that students will not know what to expect. However, as long as they are prepared to comment and compare different poems in terms of their content, theme, structure and language, students should be ready for whatever the exam can throw at them. This section is worth 20% of your total grade at GCSE.

Paper 2 itself makes up 60% of your total grade or, in other words, 96 raw marks. Just under half of those marks, 44 to be exact (27.5% of 60%), can be gained from analysing how the writer uses language, form and structure to create effects. To get a high grade, it is necessary for students to use appropriate literary terms, like metaphors, similes and so on.

AO1 accounts for 36 marks of the total of 96 (22.5% of the 60% for Paper 2, to be exact). To score highly on AO1, students need to provide an informed personal response, using quotations to support their point of view.

AO3 is all about context and, like Paper 1, only 7.5% of the total mark is awarded for this knowledge (12 marks). Similarly, AO4 (which is about spelling, punctuation and grammar) only accounts for 2.5% of the total (4 marks).

One of the difficulties with Paper 1 is the language. That can't be helped, bearing in mind that part A of the exam paper involves answering questions on Shakespeare, whereas part B is all about the 19th-century novel.

To further complicate things, the education system is in a state of flux: that means we have to be ready for constant change. Of course, everyone had got used to grades A,B and C meaning a pass. It was simple, it was straightforward and nearly everyone understood it. Please be prepared that from this day henceforward, the top grade will now be known as 9. A grade 4 will be a pass, and anything below that will be found and anything above it will be a pass. Hopefully, that's not too confusing for anyone!

Now onto the exam itself. As I said, Paper 1 consists of Shakespeare and the 19th-century novel. Like Paper 2, it is a written closed book exam (in other words you are not allowed to have the texts with you), which lasts one hour 45 minutes. You can score 64 marks, which amounts to 40% of your GCSE grade.

In section B, students will be expected to write in detail about an extract from the novel they have studied in class and then write about the novel as a whole. Just for the record, the choices of novel are the following: *The Strange Case of Dr Jekyll and Mr Hyde* by Robert Louis Stevenson, *A Christmas Carol* and *Great Expectations* by Charles Dickens, *Jane Eyre* by Charlotte Brontë, *Frankenstein* by Mary Shelley, *Pride and Prejudice* by Jane Austin, and *The Sign of Four* by Sir Arthur Conan Doyle.

Another important thing to consider is the fact that for section B of Paper 1, you will not be assessed on Assessment Objective 4 (AO4), which involves spelling, punctuation, grammar and vocabulary. This will be assessed on section A of Paper 1, which is about Shakespeare, and it will be worth 2.5% of your overall GCSE grade. In terms of raw marks, it is worth 4 out of 64. So for once, we need not concern ourselves with what is affectionately known as 'SPAG' too much on this part of Paper 1.

However, it is necessary to use the correct literary terminology wherever possible to make sure we maximise our marks on Assessment Objective2 (AO2). AO2 tests how well we can analyse language form and structure. Additionally, we are expected to state the effect the writer tried to create and how it impacts on the reader.

This brings me onto Assessment Objective 1 (AO1), which involves you writing a personal response to the text. It is important that you use quotations to backup your points of view. Like AO2, AO1 is worth 15% of your GCSE on Paper 1.

Assessment Objective 3 (AO3) is worth half of that, but nevertheless it is important to comment on context to make sure you get as much of the 7.5% up for grabs as you can.

So just to make myself clear, there are 30 marks available in section B for your answer on the 19th-century novel. Breaking it down even further, you will get 12 marks maximum the backing up your personal opinion with quotations, an additional 12 marks for analysing the writer's choice of words for effect (not forgetting to use appropriate terminology - more on that see the glossary at the back of this book), and six marks for discussing context.

As you can see, we've got a lot to get through so without further ado let's get on with the actual text itself and possible exam questions.

Previous exam questions

Notwithstanding the governmental changes to the grading system, it is still good practice to go over previous exam papers. I've looking at a specimen paper from 2014, which asks students to analyse how Ishiguro presents fear about the future in the novel,so I've deliberately mentioned this aspect as I've gone through the novel. Students are advised to look at different characters' fears about the future and expected to analyse how the writer uses language to present these ideas.

9-1 GCSE REVISION NOTES – NEVER LET ME GO

To make sure that you meet AQA's learning objectives and get a high mark, make sure you go into the exam knowing something about the following:

- the plot
- the characters
- the theme
- selected quotations/details
- exam skills

Page-by-page analysis

Chapter One

The novel begins with the short sentence: 'My name is Kathy H' (3) This seems a very simplistic way to start, but reading between the lines we can guess that the story is set in the future where surnames no longer matter. Alternatively, she could be hiding her name; for what reason, we don't know. The idea that her individuality is unimportant in the greater scheme of things comes across loud and clear.

The narrative continues in the first person ('I', 'me' and so on) and the reader gets the feeling that Kathy enjoys clarity, judging by the simple sentence structures used in the narrative.

Arguably, the most ominous word at the start is 'they' (3). This makes the reader wonder who this personal pronoun refers to. It appears that 'they' have a lot of power, as Kathy does not protest that she will have to continue as a 'carer' 'until the end of the year' (3). At this stage, we can only guess what being a 'carer' entails.

We can guess that carers help 'donors' to convalesce after surgery (3). The question is what do 'donors' donate? The writer is deliberately arousing the readers' curiosity.

It appears, if we can trust Kathy's account, that she is good at what she does. However, more questions come to mind as we discover that 'hardly any' of her donors 'have been classified as "agitated", even before the fourth donation' (3). The burning question is what is the fourth donation? The number 4 is associated with death in Japanese as it's pronounced 'shi', which sounds exactly the same as word for death. Given that the writer, Kazuo Ishiguro, was born in Japan perhaps it is not surprising that we learn later in the novel that 'the fourth donation' usually equates to death.

We also discover that Kathy is proud to be a product of 'Hailsham' and a 'calm' carer, although she claims earlier that she is 'not trying to boast' (3). The fact that she later partially retracts with the word 'maybe' shows that she is honest (3).

The reason for her modesty may be her almost inexplicable fear of 'resentment' (3). This is quite mystifying at this stage of the novel, as having a 'bedsit' does not make her sound like someone who should be envied (3). If Kathy thinks a 'bedsit' is the epitome of high living, then she must be accustomed to much worse; we begin to have some sympathy for her character (3).

Kathy certainly appears to be content, but fears 'resentment' from 'carers who 'are just as good and don't get half the credit' (3). Kathy uses direct address, which suggests she is talking to someone, when she says: 'If you're one of them [carers]' (3). It appears that she has found another carer to confide in. We can guess that this carer barely knows Kathy as it appears that she is about to tell that person her life story.

Kathy feels privileged in comparison to other carers, perhaps because she is an ex-Hailsham student. The name 'Hailsham' sounds quite harsh, so the reader may feel that Kathy is misguided in feeling so positive about her position (3). After all, 'Hail' makes us think of frozen drops of rainfall, that most of us try to escape from in the winter. Meanwhile, the word 'sham' means 'fake'. It appears that Kathy has been hoodwinked or deceived and therefore her feeling of contentment with her position is unenviable; it seems based on delusion, even if she does get to 'pick and choose' who she cares for. Nevertheless, we may accept being a Hailsham student 'is enough by itself sometimes to get people's backs up' if we believe that many other people are suffering much more than 31-year-old Kathy (3).

Although, she will have been a carer for exactly 12 years, there is little evidence that she fears for her future, at this stage in the novel. Kathy seems to stoically accept everything that is offered to her in this futuristic society.

The writer is already presenting Kathy's world as a dystopia, with 'agitated' standing out in quotation marks (3). What are donors 'agitated' about? This question gives the reader an ominous flavour of what is to come, while giving yet another reason to read on in order to find out more.

We quickly discover that Kathy is indeed 'privileged' to be 'from Hailsham' (4). Being allowed to pick and choose her donors has allowed to reunite with fellow former Hailsham students, Ruth and Tommy.

Kathy seems resigned to her fate, saying 'it feels just about right to be finishing at last come the end of the year' (4). The words 'at last' indicate she has had enough of her job. This is supported by her admission that there are 'fewer and fewer donors left' whom she remember (4). We assume, as readers, that donors are dying or disappearing somewhere. Anyway, the reader may be more worried about Kathy's future than she is, as she seems to stoically accept all that this future society is about to throw at her.

We find out that the fate of a donor seems particularly harsh. The word 'completing' appears to be a euphemism for 'dying' (5). The only consolation for this particular unnamed donor suffering 'blotches' and grimacing through his pain is Kathy's recollections of Hailsham (5). This donor does not appear to have any pleasant memories of his own, so perhaps the possible resentment of other members of this future society seem partially understandable.

We find out a bit more about Hailsham, when Kathy mentions things that remind her of the place, for instance: 'a misty field' (6). This suggests that Hailsham is a place where the truth is blurred or hidden. She reminisces about her student days as she drives 'around the country' (6).

Another thing that Kathy associates with Hailsham is 'poplar trees' (6). These trees grow quickly but do not last as long as other trees. Is this to show us how ephemeral life is for Kathy and her kind? Additionally, poplars require little care; they have to be replaced when they die. Does this tell us anything about the students at Hailsham?

Another word that stands out is 'prefab' (6). Like poplars, prefabricated housing does not last long in comparison to many other types of home. It is mildly disconcerting for the reader that Kathy finds prefabs so comforting, but it shows that her world is very different from our own, where we crave more stability and longevity.

Kathy describes the prefabs as having 'windows unnaturally high up, tucked almost under the eaves' (6). This makes the reader think of 'eaves-dropping', which is euphemism for listening to other people's conversations while staying out of sight. This is another disconcerting image, which shows an undesirable aspect of the dystopian future presented by the writer.

However, the presentation of Hailsham is not all negative. Kathy admits they 'loved' their 'sports pavilion', which makes the reader think of cricket, which is also mentioned (6). Additionally, access to a 'veranda' is difficult to view negatively (6).

We find out a little more about the other characters in the story, when Kathy mentions 'Jenny B.', who like her has an abbreviated surname (7). Perhaps neither of them has a surname at all.

It seems that the female students enjoy the 'gossip', which ties in with the image of 'eaves-dropping', already discussed (7).

The aforementioned Ruth comes across as a callous character as she describes the unsuspecting Tommy as an 'idiot' (7). Kathy describes the vague curiosity the girls feel as they 'watch' Tommy's latest humiliation unfold' (7). We have some sympathy for Tommy, who appears to be the victim here.

The cruelty of the female students is apparent in the actions of Laura, 'the big clown' in the group (8). Laura mimics Tommy, who is about to be ridiculed again. We don't know how many times this has happened, but we can guess that it has become a kind of ritual at Hailsham.

Our sympathy dissipates for Tommy somewhat when we find out he has 'plenty of [...] tantrums' (9). This suggests he has a bad temper. Nevertheless, we suspect he is mercilessly tormented, if the behaviour of Kathy's group is anything to go by. Tommy certainly seems to be a tormented soul, judging by 'the hurt and panic' Kathy can see developing on his face as he waits to be picked for one of the football teams (9). The reader has some sympathy for his plight, as Tommy is positively described as 'eager' (9). This suggests that the teasing might be completely unjustified.

Tommy is particularly ridiculed by Laura, who describes him as 'rehearsing his Shakespeare' as he flies into a rage (10). His tantrum certainly seems theatrical as when he screams he appears to look like 'a dog doing a pee' (10). Reading between the lines, this description suggests that Tommy might be as loyal as a dog, although the intention of the unknown speaker is to belittle him.

Hannah points out that Tommy is singled-out for this treatment because 'he's a layabout' (10). This does not seem to tie in with the 'eager' boy we've already heard about. We discover the 'layabout' tag comes from the fact that 'Tommy never even tried to be creative' (10). Once again, the writer has put more questions into the readers' heads, as we wonder what what 'creative' means in this dystopia. Presumably, it means students have to create something for 'the Spring Exchange', although quite what that is remains unclear at this stage (10). We can only assume that creativity is traded in this 'Exchange' (10).

Kathy admits the group she's with feel 'guilty' after taking their 'ringside seats' (10). It makes the reader feel that Kathy and the rest of the watching audience are bloodthirsty, as if they are spectators at a boxing match.

However, Kathy is different from the rest of her group. She decides to 'drift over towards him' (10). The word 'drift' suggests that Kathy had little control over her desire to help Tommy. Kathy does not even heed

'Ruth's urgent whisper' to return to the group (11). This shows that Kathy has a more independent spirit than her peers.

Kathy seems to be warm-hearted, judging by this description of her putting 'a hand on' Tommy's arm (11). This simple gesture depicts her as gentle and kind.

Tommy is out of control, as shown by his 'flailing' arms (11). He accidentally slaps Kathy in the face, as a result.

Kathy's response is to speak 'sternly' to Tommy (11). By talking like this, she appears to be like a teacher or someone else in authority. Even Kathy's patience (a necessary quality for a carer presumably) begins to wane as she admits she'd 'had enough of him' (11).

The last words of the chapter are spoken by Ruth, who refers to Tommy as a 'mad animal'. Once again, **animal imagery** is used to refer to him, showing him to be perhaps more innocent than the average human being and possibly less sophisticated.

Chapter Two

The theme of the unreliability of memory comes up at the beginning of this chapter, as Kathy admits 'I might have got some of it wrong' (13). This adds to the impression that she is modest.

We also discover that Hailsham had to undergo regular medical tests with 'stern Nurse Trisha' (13). Kathy admits that students referred to Trisha as 'Crow Face', which conveys the idea that the medical practitioner is harsh and possibly wrinkled, if she has 'crow's feet' around her eyes. No explanation of the foreboding nickname is given, but crows traditionally symbolise death.

The reader may notice water imagery used to describe Tommy 'in the stream' of students 'coming down' the stairs at Hailsham (13). The metaphor may suggest that it is difficult for the students to resist the current, or in this case going along with all the other students are doing. Nevertheless, Tommy is independent enough to resist the flow, stopping 'dead on the stairs' (13).

We discover that Kathy is quite impatient when it comes to Tommy. She even finds his 'big open smile' 'immediately irritating' (13). This does not seem to be one of the attributes you would expect of a carer. However, she is quite guarded about what she says, by not fully expressing her anger and saying instead: 'Tommy, you're holding everyone up' (13).

Kathy is forgiving as she accepts Tommy's apology whole-heartedly, saying: 'it's now one hundred per cent forgotten' (14). However, the fact she's mentioning this in the narrative suggests while she has forgiven Tommy for striking her, it is far from forgotten.

Although they are only aged 'thirteen', Tommy has already developed physically in 'size and strength' (14, 15). This makes the bullying all the more surprising, although Ruth explains that Tommy's 'attitude' and lack of contributions to the 'Spring Exchange' are the cause (15). Ruth appears to be the leader of the group, as 'everyone was waiting for Ruth's response' after Kathy opined that what was happening to Tommy it 'wasn't really very fair' (15).

Some explanations of the system at Hailsham follow, as discover that students are expected to contribute 'paintings, drawings, pottery' and so on to the 'Exchange' (16). For their efforts, 'guardians' reward students with 'Exchange Tokens' to buy other students' work (16). The word 'token' suggests this currency is meaningless and worthless. Nevertheless, Kathy explains the importance of 'building up a collection of personal possessions' in Hailsham (16).

Ruth and Kathy discuss this system, while the former is recovering from her latest donation in Dover. Ruth asserts that 'poetry's important' (17). Kathy questions the value of 'nine-year-old stuff', whereas Ruth seems to be readier to accept the rules. While the pair reflect on their lives at Hailsham, the 'gleaming white tiles' makes the place seem like 'a hall of mirrors' (17). It has been pointed out by critics, Glennis Byron and Linda Ogston, that this imagery is similar to that employed by Mary Shelley in *Frankenstein* when the monster looks at himself in a pool of water. Additionally, they point out that halls of mirrors produce endless copies, which is relevant as you will discover as you read on.

Tommy's 'deliberately not trying' is the subject the pair return to (18). This appears to have all started in 'Miss Geraldine's art classes' (19). Tommy's watercolour 'of an elephant standing in some tall grass' sparked off all the bullying, according to Kathy (19). It was intended as 'a kind of joke', but it backfired on Tommy (19).

The word 'resentment' crops up again, as Kathy reveals that the other students resented how Miss Geraldine tried 'to praise' Tommy's inadequate painting (20). The underlying feeling is most students feel they have to conform to expectations, whereas Tommy feels justified in producing 'deliberately childish' work (20).

Tommy evolves into a more mature character, as he 'somehow' controls himself, despite 'the pranks' continuing (21). Eventually, it causes the teasing to stop.

Kathy cannot figure out what has caused the change in Tommy, but is pleased with 'these developments' (22). Tommy is described in watery terms again, as he 'floated the ball across the grass' during a game of football (22). Reading between the lines, this metaphor could indicate that Tommy is floating in the environment rather than drowning.

Kathy, meanwhile, is curious about the changes in Tommy and asks him 'what's happened?' (23). Tommy tells Kathy that she's 'so nosy', before revealing that Miss Lucy's talk changed his attitude (23). Kathy reveals that she was 'genuinely angry' at what she perceives to be a lie (23). This shows that she wants to completely understand Tommy and feels short-changed.

They agree to meet by 'the pond' to discuss it further (24). Once again, Tommy is linked with water. It seems an apt place to cleanse people of their sins, if we are to read anything Biblical into the text. This may be intentional on the part of the writer, as Kathy asked Tommy if he had found 'God or something' previously (23).

Chapter Three

The chapter begins at the pond with Tommy wearing a 'maroon track suit top' (25). The adjective 'maroon' links to the verb 'marooned', which emphasises Tommy's isolation. Therefore, it's a **pun**.

Kathy's narrative then describes Miss Lucy as 'the most sporting of the guardians' (26). Miss Lucy's 'squat, almost bulldoggy figure, and her odd black hair' do not make her appear glamorous (26). However, like Tommy, she is interested in sport and she is described as being dog-like. Therefore, Tommy and Miss Lucy could be kindred spirits.

Then we discover that Miss Lucy, like the other guardians, lives in 'the Orangery' (27). This could indicate that the guardians aim to cultivate the students like oranges. Quite what will happen to the fruit of their labours is unclear at this stage.

Tommy reveals to Kathy that Miss Lucy was 'shaking' with 'rage' when they had their little talk (28). This revelation sets up another question which the reader hopes will be answered later in the novel, as it is not clear exactly why she is so angry. It does appear that Miss Lucy is a rebel, who can therefore identify with Tommy who was struggling to conform.

The theme of education and ignorance is touched on as Tommy reveals that Miss Lucy believes the students are not 'being taught enough' (29). Kathy claims they have been 'taught' about donations, but Tommy seems confused about it.

Like the students, the reader is being kept in the dark about a lot of what is really going on at Hailsham, so experiences some of the same feeling vicariously. The next question to pop up is 'why does Madame' take their best pictures for 'the Gallery'? (30).

Kathy's narrative partially explains what the Gallery is. We discover it is a taboo subject and 'there was an unspoken rule' that students must not mention it (31). This shows how afraid they are: not of the future particularly, but more of the present.

We find out more about **Madame's character** as she is described as 'French or Belgian', 'tall, narrow [...] with short hair' (32). Madame's business-like appearance is emphasised by her 'sharp grey suit' (32). Madame has a 'chilly look' that makes her seem unapproachable. Interestingly, she is a female character who may have been married, as 'Madame' is French for 'Mrs'.

Ruth shows some originality of thought by suggesting that Madame is 'scared' of the students (33). The 'billiards room' is used to exhibit the best work of the students, which suggests that like billiards, the exhibition is an elaborate game (33).

Kathy states 'a car was a rarity', which shows how isolated Hailsham is (34). When Madame's car appears it creates 'bedlam' in the classroom (34). This is an oblique **Biblical reference**, as bedlam refers to the nickname of a madhouse in Victorian London called the Hospital of St Mary of Bethlehem. Of course, this refers to Jesus Christ's mother. Yet, despite the religious name, the hospital that dealt with mental patients became notorious for treating the inmates poorly. This suggests something just as awful is going on at Hailsham, and that despite all its grand intentions, it's a place full of pretences.

We discover that Ruth is right in her assumption that Madame is scared of the students. The students enact their plan, deciding to 'swarm out', implying they are behaving like annoying insects (34). To Madame, the students do appear like insects, as she suppresses 'a shudder' (35). Kathy compares Madame's reaction to someone being 'afraid of spiders' (35).

Kathy admits that at the time they did not realise the implications of what had happened with Madame, although they knew they were 'different' from the guardians and the people outside Hailsham (36). Once again, direct address is used, giving the impression that Kathy is confiding in a donor or a carer: 'I'm sure somewhere in your childhood, you too had an experience like ours' (36). The use of 'you' draws the reader in, inviting him or her to find similar experiences to compare to Kathy's to make identification with the character even stronger.

Chapter Four

Kathy begins this chapter claiming that the 'urge' to 'order' all her memories has been sparked by the need to prepare for the forthcoming 'change of pace' (37). She seems to have no fear of the future, for she says: 'I'll welcome the chance to rest' (37). Despite the fact that she 'won't be a carer any more [sic]', Kathy seems unperturbed by whatever awaits her (37). It seems as if she is sick of being a carer and wants to move onto the next stage of her life. She appears ready to embrace that change.

Next, we hear about the 'token controversy' (38). It seems like questioning the rationale of Hailsham's conventions is in itself controversial. The reader gets the idea that the only acceptable position for a student is to accept his or her fate stoically; in that sense, Kathy appears to be close to being an ideal student.

The idea that students should be compensated for their work is put forward by Roy J. to **Miss Emily**. We now find out that Miss Emily is the 'head guardian' (39). Miss Emily's 'silvery hair' is 'tied back' (39). Like Madame, Miss Emily seems aloof, with her loose strands of hair remaining 'beneath her contempt' (39).

Nevertheless, the portrayal is not all negative, as Kathy reports that students considered Miss Emily 'to be fair' (39). Although Miss Emily's presence is 'intimidating', she makes the students 'feel so safe' (39). Miss Emily has a 'quiet, deliberate voice', which possibly has a calming effect on the students (39).

Roy's meeting with Miss Emily results in some tokens being awarded to students, 'but not many because it was a "most distinguished honour" to have work selected by Madame' for the Gallery' (39). The row rumbles on, consequently, with Polly T. asking Miss Lucy why Madame takes students' 'things anyway?' (40). . Miss Lucy replies that 'it's for a good reason' (40). Polly has broken an 'unwritten rule' by asking the question (40). It is yet another taboo area for students, who are expected to accept rules at face value; they are discouraged from asking important questions.

Kathy goes on to explain the excitement surrounding the 'Sales' (41). Unlike the 'Exchanges', students would use their tokens for 'renewing stuff that was wearing out or broken' (41). This foreshadows the fate of the donors whose organs are used as spare parts for others in this dystopia. However, at this stage in the narrative, the reader is not completely aware of the details. The grim future that awaits donors is only hinted at.

Although Kathy calls the Sales 'a big disappointment', she reveals that 'things would get out of hand' in the frenzied excitement (41, 42). The punishment for students would be a sit-down assembly with 'no announcements, just Miss Emily talking' (42). Kathy reveals that there was something 'steely' about Miss Emily 'on these occasions' (42). Additionally, Miss Emily's 'frosty eye' makes the head guardian appear to be aloof and cold (42).

Kathy admits most of Miss Emily's words 'became a fog' (43). Her former fellow student, Ruth, looks back in retrospect, remarking that 'in a classroom' Miss Emily 'could be as clear as anything' (43). This suggests that Miss Emily is being deliberately unclear in her twenty to thirty minute speeches. We can only assume that Miss Emily wants to control the students with veiled threats, without revealing too much to them about their position in the world.

Kathy reveals that she spotted Miss Emily 'wandering around Hailsham in a dream, talking to herself' (43). This suggests that that the head is confused herself about her role in educating the students and is feeling the burden of her responsibilities.

Ruth contests this, denying that Miss Emily was 'potty' (43). Ruth adds that 'Miss Emily had an intellect you could slice logs with' (43). The suggestion here is that Miss Emily's intellect is something to be feared. Kathy admits that Miss Emily 'could be uncannily sharp' (43). The 'uncanny' is an aspect often explored in **gothic** literature, so in that sense Miss Emily is an archetype of that genre of fiction.

There is a similarity between Miss Emily and Tommy, as we discover she 'had gone into one of her rages'. Unlike, Tommy though, Miss Emily's outbursts are much quieter. Miss Emily would 'narrow her eyes' and 'whisper furiously to herself' (43). Once again, we get the impression she is struggling with the burden of responsibility. Additionally, we get the idea that she is keeping secrets from the students as she cannot speak plainly about why she is disappointed with their behaviour. disappointment. However, according to Kathy, students feel that they 'have fallen' in Miss Emily's 'estimation' if they do something wrong, and that feeling is awful enough for them to want to do something to 'redeem' themselves (44). From that, you get the distinct impression that Kathy cares deeply about what the guardians think of her.

Kathy reveals that she caught Miss Emily 'talking under her breath, pointing and directing remarks to an invisible audience' (45). Miss Emily looks 'straight at' Kathy while 'mouthing her address' (45). This suggests that Miss Emily could be a machine, as Miss Emily 'never mentioned' the incident and is clearly not disturbed by Kathy's presence(45). Either that or Miss Emily's concentration level is inhuman. Another possibility is that Miss Emily is extremely short-sighted. The narrative is providing the reader with more questions to ponder.

We next find out a bit more about Ruth and her imaginary horses. In a place so fraught with danger, perhaps it is no surprise that she has named two of her horses 'Thunder', which foreshadows a storm to come, and 'Bramble', an encounter which sounds quite painful if taken literally. Ruth allows Kathy to ride 'Bramble', as long as she does not use her 'crop on him' (46). The word 'crop' has already been used to describe the Sales: the words 'A real bumper crop' would bring 'a thrilled cheer' from the students (42). This relates to the idea that the students will be harvested like crops, as we shall see later.

Kathy accepts 'the invisible rein' offered by Ruth 'at the wire mesh boundary' (47). It appears that the students' live are controlled by invisible strings, as if they are puppets; they are not wild horses who can run free. Indeed, they are more like flowers, whose growth is carefully controlled by gardeners. Perhaps that is why Ruth names one of her horses 'Daffodil' (47).

The discussion between Ruth and Kathy moves on to Miss Geraldine. Kathy admits that Miss Geraldine is her 'favourite' guardian (48). Consequently, Ruth allows Kathy to become one of Miss Geraldine's 'secret guards' (48). As with her horses, the guards appear to be a figment of Ruth's fertile imagination. Quite why a guardian needs guarding appears unclear, at this stage. The role reversal shows that Ruth feels frustration at being powerless. Ruth appears to have an urge to guard others, rather than being guarded herself. Interestingly, continuing the play on words, the guardians all appear to be guarded in their responses so far: no one is able to reveal the whole truth about the students and their future.

Chapter Five

We now discover that Ruth believes there is a 'plot to kidnap Miss Geraldine'; the secret guards will have to thwart it as they are sworn to 'protect her' (49). Kathy reveals that Ruth is the 'leader' of the guards, although she is not sure if she was the originator or not (49).

The secret guards feel sure that the 'dark fringe of trees' that lie 'at the top of the hill' will have something to do with the plot (49). The students appear to be scared of nature, as Kathy mentions her fear of hearing 'the wind rustling the branches' at night (50).The students even punish Marge K., by making her stare at the woods. It is as though, the natural world and the truth it represents is to be feared. The students appear to be feel safer in their more unnatural surroundings, where ignorance is bliss.

Looking back retrospectively, Kathy casts aspersion about the 'evidence' accumulated by the students about who is in the plot to kidnap Miss Geraldine (51). Unsuprisingly, the unpopular Miss Eileen is implicated, as is Mr Roger, who is caught conferring 'furtively' with the former (51).

Like the guardians, Ruth controls her group by manipulating information: she keeps her edge over the others by implying she knows more than she does. Kathy reveals that if Ruth 'sensed opposition, she'd just allude darkly to stuff she knew "from before"' (52).

The theme of education is alluded to as Kathy reveals Ruth's mistaken belief that all pieces in chess move in 'an L-shape' (53). As well as 'learner', perhaps 'L' can refer to limited knowledge. Ruth is adamant that she is right about the rules of chess, but Kathy's superior knowledge results in her 'storming off' (53). The game of chess is like the students' lives, in that they are trying to conform to rules with varying degrees of success.

Kathy's inability to follow Ruth's rules of chess end up with her being expelled from the 'secret guard'. However, Kathy takes umbrage when Moira claims the 'whole secret guard thing' is 'stupid' (54). Kathy's urge to be back in the group causes her to feel 'furious' (54). Kathy has no desire to team up with Moira, who has been ostracised for much longer. It appears that for the students, there is strength in numbers or at least comfort from contact with peers.

Kathy reflects that the anger emanates from her fear of crossing 'some line' (55). The word 'some' suggests that Kathy's idea of boundaries is vague. However, she does feel 'loyalty' towards Ruth, and that is an admirable quality that most readers will identify with. Nevertheless, the reader may feel it is disconcerting that Kathy would rather avoid the truth than fall out with her friends.

Ruth continues to try to manipulate Kathy. Touching on the theme of education, Ruth's 'pencil case' assumes great importance for Kathy (56). The pencil case is described as 'like a polished shoe' with 'circled red dots drifting all over it' (56). Additionally, it has a 'furry pom-pom' zip (56). It seems very elaborate, a bit like Ruth's lies. Then, according to Kathy, Ruth implies that Miss Geraldine gave it to her as 'a gift' (56). Quite how Kathy arrives at this conclusion is a little mystifying, but Ruth's 'knowing smile' appears to have allowed Kathy to read between the lines (56). The reader is not sure if Kathy's interpretation is correct, as Ruth only says: 'Let's *agree* I got it in the Sales' (56). The word 'agree' is italicised, giving it greater emphasis. This shows that Ruth expects all her follower to agree with her interpretation of events, but it is clear that since the chess game, Kathy is developing her own notions of truth. In short, Kathy may be becoming too uncontrollable to be in Ruth's group.

Kathy spends time thinking about the pencil case and believes that 'a present like that was so beyond the bounds' (57). She has a clearer idea than Ruth about what is acceptable in Hailsham. In comparison, Ruth seems hell-bent on testing the invisible boundaries set by the guardians. This puts conventional Kathy in opposition to the more revolutionary Ruth.

Consequently, Kathy hatches a plan to expose Ruth's lie. Kathy plans to access the 'registers kept of everything bought at the Sales' (58). Kathy eventually realises it is not necessary to execute the plan fully in order to achieve the desired result. Instead, Kathy intends to use 'bluff' (59).

Using the pathetic fallacy of 'the rain suddenly' getting 'heavier', the writer signals that something awful is about to happen in the narrative (59). By allowing Ruth between the lines, Kathy makes her incredibly 'upset' (59). Small items mean a lot to the students, it seems.

Ruth's reaction is to walk 'off into the rain' (60). This signifies that Ruth is more content living in her dream. Kathy's comparative clarity has disturbed Ruth to the core.

Chapter Six

The offending pencil case 'vanished from view' (61). This shows how embarrassed Ruth is at being found out. Kathy tries and succeeds in boosting Ruth's shattered confidence by saying: 'If Ruth goes and asks Miss Geraldine, then we'd stand a chance [of being allowed outside in the rain]' (61). Kathy is clearly adept at reestablishing the equilibrium by massaging egos. This may be a useful skill for a carer.

Midge brings up the new taboo subject of Ruth's pencil case, asking where it is and calling it 'luscious' (62). Ruth's reply is that she keeps the pencil case in her 'collection chest', which resembles a coffin judging by the previous description of 'a wooden chest with your name on it' (62, 38). The inevitable conclusion is that Ruth's dream of achieving closer relationship with her favourite guardian Geraldine has died.

Kathy uses this opportunity to become more like a guardian as Midge continues to probe. Kathy replies: 'There are some very good reasons why we can't tell you where it came from' (63). Kathy 'gives' Midge 'a smile', which may sound condescending to the reader but appears completely acceptable in the dystopian world that the characters live in.

We then find out about Kathy's favourite album, entitled *Songs After Dark* by Judy Bridgewater. As well as the recurring water motif, the fictional singer's name implies crossing a natural boundary created by a river or lake (64). Somehow, we expect Kathy to venture outside Hailsham's expectations of her somewhere later on in the narrative.

That important moment has to wait, as Kathy instead reveals how the students learn to think of Norfolk as 'a lost corner' where 'lost property was kept' (65). Although Miss Emily has not said it during the lesson, the students have added two and two together to make twenty-two. This shows the power and danger of imagination.

Kathy admits the students' belief in Norfolk becomes 'a real source of comfort' (66). So when Kathy's lost tape turns up in that county, she feels 'some old wish to believe again in something' (66). The students seems to derive pleasure from wishful thinking, sometimes disregarding the facts in order to cling on to reassuring ideas.

To Kathy, Judy Bridgewater represents rebellion. On the album cover, the singer has 'a cigarette burning in her hand' (67). Smoking is outlawed at Hailsham, so even entertaining notions of using tobacco is taboo. Clearly, Kathy enjoys the escapism represented by Bridgwater in her 'purple satin dress' with palm trees behind her and 'swarthy waiters in white tuxedos' (67).

Nevertheless, Kathy and her fellow students seem deeply shocked when Miss Lucy reveals that she 'did smoke for a little while' when she was 'younger' (68). Unlike them, Miss Lucy is not *special*, so keeping 'heathy inside' is not as important (68). Miss Lucy's revelations are uncomfortably truthful for the students, who appear to be happier to drift through the fog of lies at Hailsham provided by most of their guardians. Perhaps the guardians are protecting the students from the grisly truth.

Kathy mentions the 'donations waiting' for them (69). By the use of personification, the writer has made the donations appear even more threatening to the students. This increases the sense of foreboding building in the reader.

Perhaps the climactic moment in the novel is where Kathy reveals her own imagining, while listening to *Never Let Me Go*. She would 'imagine' that the words were about 'a woman who'd been told she couldn't have babies'. This infertile woman 'has a baby, and she holds this baby very close to her and walks around singing: "Baby never let me go"' (70).

Kathy reveals she 'was swaying about slowly in time to the song, holding an imaginary baby' when she catches sight of 'Madame framed in the doorway' (71). The reader gets the idea that Kathy cannot have babies, as Madame is 'crying' (71). Additionally, the reader has some sympathy for Madame, who clearly feels more than her earlier aloofness suggests.

The information hinted at is confirmed as Kathy reveals: 'none of us could have babies' (72). She adds: 'None of us [...] was particularly bothered' (72). Once again, it appears that the students stoically accept their future; they rarely want to challenge what they are told.

Nevertheless, Kathy's holding of an imaginary baby is subconsciously rebellious. Consequently, her music tape disappears after Madame observes Kathy in the middle of the performance. Kathy strangely 'never linked' the disappearance of the tape with Madame's discovery, although there was only a couple of months separating the 'two events' (73). This shows how naive Kathy is, as even in retrospect she cannot believe that the guardians would raid her collection chest to preserve relative harmony at Hailsham.

However, in retrospect Kathy can admit 'there was more thieving going on at Hailsham than we - or the guardians - ever wanted to admit' (74). Nevertheless, Kathy still manages to turn that event into something positive, as she relates that the 'tape disappearing' gave Ruth the opportunity to do 'something nice' (74).

Ruth tries unsuccessfully to replace the lost tape with 'Twenty Classic Dance Tunes' (75). Nevertheless, Kathy is gratified. She admits she feels 'the disappointment ebbing away and being replaced by a real happiness' (75). By using water imagery in the word 'ebbing', the writer shows how emotional Kathy was about Ruth's gesture. We wonder whether she is close to crying watery tears.

Chapter Seven

The narrative moves to the period when Kathy was aged between 'thirteen' and when she 'left at sixteen' (76). She calls these years 'darker', presumably because she becomes more aware of the uncomfortable truth. Kathy certainly has more questions to ask and some answers may be provided by Miss Lucy, 'the most likely source of important clues' (76).

Miss Lucy reveals during a lesson about World War Two prison camps that she is glad the 'fences at Hailsham aren't electrified' (77). Miss Lucy mentions 'terrible accidents' which fill the reader and the students with a sense of dread (77). She says no more about it, as if what has happened is unspeakably awful. In this way, Miss Lucy's outburst conforms to the conventions of the gothic.

The simile 'like a crouching animal waiting to pounce' describes Miss Lucy in a more threatening way (78). However, the reader feels some sympathy for the guardian, as she is described with her head 'bent down just a little too far' (78). Kathy notes there is something 'odd' about Miss Lucy's 'posture' (78). The reader can only speculate as to the cause. Perhaps Miss Lucy is weighed down by the responsibility of being a guardian and having to be guarded about the truth.

Miss Lucy interrupts Peter J., who is voicing his ambition to be an actor. She replies: 'If no one else will talk to you [...] then I will' (79). Miss Lucy is breaking ranks with her colleagues and seems to be putting her job on the line.

Miss Lucy is the most lucid of all the guardians, hence the name. She tells the students in no uncertain terms: 'none of you will be film stars' (80). More disturbingly, she informs them that they'll 'start to donate' their 'vital organs' before they are 'even middle-aged' (80).

Kathy reveals that she had some 'vague' notions about donations prior to Miss Lucy's outburst (81). However, Kathy feels the guardians 'managed to smuggle into' their 'heads a lot of the basic facts about' their 'futures' without them being fully cognisant of them (81). This was partly achieved by combining sex education with 'talk about the donations' (81). With students' attention mostly focused on sex, the guardians are able to lecture about donations without dealing with awkward questions.

Miss Emily seems to be discouraging the students from engaging in sexual activity, by demonstrating with a 'skeleton' and a 'pointer' during 'sex lectures' (82). The use of a skeleton makes the students associate sex and possibly pleasure with death.

Kathy admits: 'we still didn't discuss donations' (83). The students' fate is just another topic to avoid. She admits they made 'jokes' about it (83). It seems that the students have a dark sense of humour. Perhaps that is the only way they can deal with their lack of a future.

When Christopher H. claims that Tommy's gash on his elbow might '*unzip*', it sounds as if the students may be androids (84). It turns out that the students are bandying about another fiction, just to irritate Tommy, who is naive enough to believe it.

The theme of education is touched upon again, as Tommy reveals his concern that he will wake up to 'find his whole upper arm and hand skeletally exposed, the skin flopping about next to him "like one of those long gloves in *My Fair Lady*"' (85). The film *My Fair Lady* is a musical adaptation of George Bernard Shaw's *Pygmalion*, which deals with the education of a young working-class woman so she can mix with higher society. This intertextuality invites comparisons with the novel, as there is an even more rigid class system present at work in this dystopia than there is in *My Fair Lady* and *Pygamalion*. The reason why becomes more apparent later.

Kathy reveals that 'unzipping' becomes 'a running joke', as students use the idea to put each other off their food (86). This morbid sense of humour is perhaps how students deal with their lack of a future. They seem firmly anchored in the present.

In retrospect as he reflects on his life, Tommy realises that as students they were too self-centred to stop 'to think' (87). Rather than the unzipping, Tommy is referring to the 'troubled' Miss Lucy's feelings.

Chapter Eight

The reader expects to discover the truth, as the writer uses the pathetic fallacy of the 'brilliant sunshine' to reveal something about Miss Lucy (88).

The writer uses 'a hissing noise' to create a disconcerting atmosphere (88). The first thing that comes to mind is a snake, so the reader feels something threatening is about to appear.

We soon discover the source of the hissing: Miss Lucy 'scrawling furious lines over a page with a pencil' (89). It appears that this particular guardian has had enough of the boundaries set at Hailsham and is cracking up under the strain.

After discovering the source of the sound, Kathy goes 'down the staircase burning with shame and resentment' (90). It is almost as if Kathy is descending into her own personal hell. Quite why she feels 'shame' and 'resentment' is hard to fathom. Kathy admits she felt very 'confused', which is easier to understand. Perhaps Kathy is ashamed to find out that her guardian is so emotionally frail, as it implies that Hailsham is not all that seems to be. Maybe she resents that Miss Lucy has brought the truth uncomfortably close and made it harder to ignore.

The students feel much more comfortable with lies and half-truths. For example, Laura pretends a 'chunk of mud stuck' on Tommy's back is 'poo-poo' (91). The word 'poo-poo' shows how immature Laura is. Tommy shows his increasing maturity by 'abruptly' stalking off, instead of losing his temper in the face of this latest round of teasing (91).

Tommy is next found 'beside the big sycamore', a tree which symbolises life (92). He seems in a good mood, until Kathy produces 'Patricia's calendar' (92). This appears to remind Tommy that he is incapable of producing 'creative' sketches that rank with Patricia's, so he marches off (92).

Kathy then comments on the genuine nature of Tommy's romantic involvement with Ruth as, compared to Sylvia B. and Roger D., they are not 'stomach-churning' (93). Kathy adds that the guardians' sex lessons contain contradictory information. The result is confusion.

We find out that 'umbrella sex' is a strange euphemism for gay sex. Kathy adds: 'I don't know how it was where you were' (94). This indicates that the listener has had a similar experience as a student, albeit not at Hailsham.

As Kathy discusses sex, we realise that '*hinting*' is more important than the real thing (95). There is a lot of nodding 'knowingly', but the irony is at Hailsham there is a scarcity of actual knowledge among the students (95).

Kathy's biggest worry is that she'll be 'all right physically' if she engages in sexual activity (96). Therefore, she choose Harry C., who appears to be 'quiet and decent' (96). Her other fears are gossip and being 'ripped apart' (96).

There is more intertextuality as Kathy reveals the books they had at Hailsham included Thomas Hardy, Edna O'Brien and Margaret Drabble. Kathy calls Hardy's novels 'more or less useless' if you are using them to educate yourself about sex. However, Hardy's novels were severely censored at the time of publication. Likewise, O'Brien's writings causes outrage for the frank way sex was discussed. All three authors use female protagonists, like Ishiguro, so perhaps that is the reason for the writer including them in Hailsham's book list.

Another relevant piece of art to Hailsham students is the film *The Great Escape* (97). Clearly, they want to keep watching the Steve McQueen scene where he jumps over the barbed wire with his motorbike because they harbour a desire to do the same.

Chapter Nine

It seems that Hailsham students thought Kathy was 'Ruth's "natural successor' when the latter 'split' with Tommy (98). Kathy appears to be easily influenced, as she admit that 'afterwards' she found herself 'thinking a lot about it' (98).

The writer uses an irony to compare Ruth to a 'spare part' without Tommy (99). This reminds the reader that Ruth will be considered as more as a sum of spare parts than as a whole person once she becomes a donor. Even at Hailsham, she is defined by her love for Tommy.

Being with others appears to be one of the school's unwritten rules. The communal spirit that pervades Hailsham is obvious when the students gather around 'a single Walkman, passing the headset around' (100). Once again, the students are testing the boundaries, as the guardians have discouraged them from participating in this practice as they fear it will 'spread ear infections' (101).

Staying on the subject of body parts, Ruth says Tommy respects Kathy because she has 'got guts' (102). Ironically, those guts will be spilled when Kathy becomes a donor.

Kathy is asked by Ruth to approach Tommy about the split. Ruth hopes she can get her boyfriend back. Kathy approaches Tommy when he is practising his football skills. Using football terminology, the writer describes how Kathy breaks 'the deadlock' by talking first (103). This shows that Kathy has set foot in Tommy's world, represented by the South Playing

Field. Luckily for her, Tommy still exudes his customary 'eagerness' (103).

Kathy looks down on Tommy, as she believes his unconvincing attempts at 'bonhomie' only advertise 'what a child' he is still is (104). She incorrectly assumes he is 'falling apart' because of Ruth, when Miss Lucy is the real cause.

More morbid thoughts come to mind, as Kathy describes the time in the afternoon 'when the lessons were finished but there was still some time to go until supper' as the 'dead hour' (105). Death appears to haunt the students every day; it is even unofficially in their timetables.

However, Tommy, like the rest of the students, is unperturbed by that. However, Tommy is upset that Miss Lucy has called his artwork 'evidence' (106). Miss Lucy's U-turn sees her claim that 'Madame's gallery' is 'important' too (106).

Tommy feels acutely embarrassed that Miss Lucy felt the need to hug him and tell him to make up for 'lost time' creatively (107). Nevertheless, he confides in Kathy, who remembers that she must try to get him to reunite with Ruth.

Tommy says that he has 'to think about the next move really carefully' (108). He reminds Kathy that they are going to be leaving Hailsham 'soon' (108). Kathy's reply is to sit 'there tugging away at the clovers' (108). This suggests an over-reliance on lucky clovers and, in other words, fate.

By the end of the chapter, Kathy finds out that Miss Lucy has 'left Hailsham' and won't be returning (109). She sets off to tell Tommy, but it seems he has already got the news as his eyes are described as 'empty' (109). Kathy implies that this event may have prompted Tommy to get back again with Ruth (109).

Chapter Ten

Part two of the novel begins with Kathy mentioning her long drives and her essay topic at Hailsham: 'Victorian novels' (113). This is apt for she has already mentioned Victorian novelist Thomas Hardy and perhaps now she is mature enough to understand his writing better. As in Hailsham, many Victorian novels are preoccupied with death and repressed sexuality.

Once again, poplars are mentioned, symbolising the students' brief lives. We can only assume that the students sent to 'Poplar Farm' became donors soonest (114). Meanwhile, Kathy is fortunate enough to be sent to The Cottages.

It seems that The Cottages are a halfway house between Hailsham and the real world. At The Cottages, 'there'd be no more guardians', so they students had to look after each other (115).

After being caged behind a fence for so long, the students are reluctant to take their first steps into freedom. Kathy admits: 'we rarely stepped beyond the confines of the Cottages' (116).

Freedom does not mean a clearer view of the future, for Kathy grows her hair 'long', so it is 'always falling across' her 'vision' (117). It is almost as if she prefers everything to be veiled, as that is what she has grown accustomed to.

Kathy admits that despite their change in circumstances, students remain 'fearful of the world'; they hang on to one another because they are 'unable quite to let each other go' (118).

They are able, however, to learn new 'mannerisms' from the television (118). A strange gesture is learned by Ruth from the veteran students: slapping 'your partner's arm near the elbow' to say goodbye (119). It shows that Ruth lacks confidence as she feels an urge to follow meaningless fads.

Kathy, by contrast, is immersed in heavy Victorian literature like George Eliot's Daniel Deronda. However, even that is somewhat devalued by Kathy's admission that how well you were settling was determined by 'how many books you'd read (120). Then again, Daniel Deronda is extremely long, so Kathy is opting for quality over the quantity of books.

Ruth's copycat tendency is revealed as she opts to read the same book as Kathy, who worries about her friend's habit of being a plot spoiler. So Kathy asks Ruth why she has adopted the same arm-hitting gesture as the veterans at The Cottages. Ruth shrugs it off as 'no big deal' (121).

Nevertheless, it sparks off a huge row. Ruth accuses Kathy of never talking 'to anyone unless they're Hailsham' (122). This implies that Kathy is snobbish or shy.

Kathy ends the chapter by picking up her book and walking off 'without another word' (123). This seems to indicate that Ruth got the better of these exchange.

Chapter Eleven

The chapter begins by outlining the content of the talks between Ruth and Kathy at the top of the alliterative 'Black Barn' (124). Kathy mentions that confidences between the two had been honoured 'until the afternoon of the Daniel Deronda business' (124). Breaches of trust also exist in the George Eliot novel, which may partly explain it being brought up again.

We find out more about Kathy as she explains how she 'planned' her sex life in The Cottages (125). This shows her calculating side. However, she is quite flexible, as she has 'a few one-nighters' instead of following her plan to 'become part of a couple with someone' (125).

Kathy confides in Ruth that 'sex has done funny things to her feelings, just as Miss Emily had warned' (126). Through Kathy, we see Ruth 'at her best: encouraging, funny, tactful, wise' (126).

The gothic idea of the doppelgänger is explored as Kathy reveals there are 'two quite separate Ruths' (127). Like a Jekyl and Hyde type characters, Ruth's dark side puts 'on airs' and pretends (127). Fortunately for Kathy, Ruth can also be the opposite of that description.

The description of Ruth's character goes deeper, as Kathy compares her friend to a performer. In Kathy's view, she has to act as if she's 'in the front row of the audience when she [Ruth] was performing on stage' (128).

Ruth has the ability to shock Kathy, as she reveals she put her collection of items accumulated at Hailsham 'in a bin bag' (129). Ruth is implying that everything taught at Hailsham is valueless and this is backed up by Keffers, who tells her: 'no shop her knew would want stuff like that' (129). The tough-talking Keffers does have a sympathetic side to his character, saying: 'I'll take it along to the Oxfam people' (129).

Although life in The Cottages is different to Hailsham, the 'misted-up windows' remind the reader of the lack of clarity endured by students at the latter place (130). Once again, there are subjects you should not talk about, for instance: 'you didn't mention these trips [veterans going on a course] out in the open' (130). Kathy stops short of calling it 'an actual taboo' as she states: 'If they had to be mentioned, they got mentioned' (130). Nevertheless, the general impression is the students are only slightly freer in this new environment.

For example, Keffers appears to frown on sexuality, going 'blotchy with fury' if he glimpsed any pornographic magazines (131). Kathy describes Keffers as 'truly scary' when in this mood (131).

Kathy's attitude to pornographic magazines is unusual, as she admits she scans the people in them 'focusing on the faces' (132). The reason for that is revealed later in the narrative, but for now the writer successfully arouses the readers' curiosity. If we take Kathy wanting 'the light' metaphorically, it appears that she is searching for the truth (133).

Tommy catches Kathy going through the pornographic magazines and observes that she has 'a strange face' (134). He also notices that she is 'sad' and 'scared' (134). From Tommy's observations the reader can tell that Kathy is deeply affected emotionally by what she is looking at. The readers expect to find out more about Kathy's reactions to pornography on the 'Norfolk trip', as the writer successfully leaves the readers on a cliff-hanger (135).

Chapter Twelve

Kathy starts the chapter by explaining the reason behind the Norfolk trip, to a 'town called Cromer' on the coast (136). Ruth reveals that the veterans, Chrissie and Rodney, have spotted a person in an office who looks like 'a possible' for her (136). At this stage, the reader can only guess what 'a possible' actually means to Ruth. Once again, the writer is engaging the readers' curiosity.

It turns out that 'possibles' were a taboo subject at Hailsham. At the Cottages, it is a little bit less out of bounds. Kathy describes these discussions as 'a world away from' arguments about the twentieth-century novelist 'James Joyce' (137). This another example of intertextuality in the novel.

Kathy then explains how 'each of' the students were 'copied at some point from a normal person' (137). She goes on to detail how 'in theory, you'd be able to find the person you were modelled from' (137). That's why all the students are keeping 'an eye out for "possibles"' (137). The 'possibles' would normally be 'twenty to thirty years older', so by looking at them students would 'glimpse' their 'future' (137).

We find out that there are two schools of thought: one that believes 'possibles' are 'an irrelevance'; and another that believes the opposite (138). Ruth, apparently, has always believed, like Kathy, that 'possibles' are just 'a technical necessity' (138). However, she seems to entertain more romantic notions now.

Whether Ruth can trust Chrissie seems doubtful, given that Kathy ominously describes the latter as 'more like the Wicked Witch than a movie star' (139). Other warning signs are Chrissie's 'irritating way of jabbing you with a finger' and 'the way she always seemed to want to separate us' (139).

Kathy reveals her doubts about the story centre around the woman being described matching too closely 'Ruth's "dream future"' (140). She believes that Chrissie is 'up to something' (140).

If we interpret the 'boxy gas heaters' metaphorically, perhaps we can assume that the sighting of the 'possible' is all hot air, lacking in substantial evidence (141). The writer uses the pathetic fallacy of 'a bitterly cold spell' to indicate that Ruth may be disappointed (141).

Ruth seems to have a photographic memory as she recalls an old image of 'dynamic, go-ahead' types in an office setting (142). Clearly, Ruth see herself fitting into this type of environment, so these words reflect how she sees herself.

At the end of the chapter, Chrissie is described as 'awestruck about' the Hailsham students 'for all her patronising manner' (143). Kathy explains how 'in some mysterious way, a separate set of rules applied' to Hailsham students (143). This is why the impossible is possible, when it comes to Ruth's 'possible' working in an office. In other words, Ruth and Kathy are part of an edit as far as the other students at the Cottages are concerned.

Chapter Thirteen

Ruth has (up until now) pretended that 'she wasn't very serious about the prospect of finding her "possible"' (144). Now we discover her other side, as she leans forward in the car as they drive towards Norfolk, 'her face stuck between the two front seats' (145). From her actions, she seems as eager as Tommy earlier in the narrative.

Ruth is quite literally at the edge of precipice, as the writer describes the group choosing a table 'closest to the cliff edge' (146). Her hopes of finding her 'possible' hang by a slender thread and this is represented metaphorically by her precarious position near the edge of a cliff.

Kathy returns to the subject of 'the near-taboo at the Cottages surrounding people who'd left' (147). She suggests that Chrissie and Rodney can only talk freely about Martin, a former veteran, now that they are away from the Cottages.

Despite being a reasonable distance away in Norfolk, Kathy still wants to comply with the rules of the Cottages. Chrissie admits visiting carers, in this case Martin, is 'not encouraged' (148). Rodney agrees that a visit would be 'naughty', but clearly both of them are determined to see their old friend despite the rules (148). Ruth adds that: 'Kathy hates to be naughty' (148). In other words, Kathy is a conformist.

Chrissie, in comparison, is a rule-breaker. Building up Ruth's hopes, at the same time, Chrissie insists that if the later works in an office (instead of becoming a carer and then a donor) she doesn't 'see how anyone' can 'stop' them 'visiting' (149). Chrissie and Rodney agree that because Ruth is an ex-Hailsham student, this impossible dream may be possible, and she cites a couple of examples to prove her point.

Tommy wants to know which one became a park keeper, but Kathy shoots him 'a warning glance' and later makes him feel stupid for asking the question (150). From this, it is clear that Tommy has the more inquiring mind. He does not want to pretend he is 'in the know' when he is not.

Chrissie mentions 'a deferral', which may be possible for ex-Hailsham students 'so long as' they 'qualified'. Using educational terminology, the writer has got the reader thinking about ignorance again. At this stage, the reader does not know exactly what these words mean in the context of the dystopia. We can only guess that deferral means putting off becoming a donor, but it could mean something else, at this stage in the narrative. The word 'qualified' is harder to work out, but most will guess it has something to do with the gallery and creativity. By setting up puzzles, the writer keeps the reader engaged.

We do feel suspicious of Chrissie's motives when she pauses and looks at each of them, 'maybe for dramatic effect' (151). Nevertheless, she continued by saying that a deferral is possible 'if you were a boy and a girl, and you were in love with each other, really' (151). We can't be sure if she's telling the truth, lying deliberately, or passing off lies as the truth as she doesn't know any better.

Another word from the world of education crops up as Rodney suddenly asks Ruth: 'Who did they say you had to go to if you wanted, you know, to apply' (152). To Ruth, it is very important to seem to be knowledgeable so she avoids answering the question.

Instead, Ruth rounds on Tommy, who says he doesn't 'remember anything like that at Hailsham' (152). She tells the others that Tommy 'isn't like a real Hailsham student' to keep her pride about where she was educated in place.

It seems the conversation is not close enough to the truth, for Kathy observes the group 'through one of the big misty windows', which metaphorically suggests ideas and visions are blurred (153). She has 'been put in charge of the spending money', so she clearly is a comparatively responsible person.

Chapter Fourteen

Through the pathetic fallacy of the sun 'hardly' penetrating, the writer sets up the reader to expect disappointment in Ruth's quest to find her 'possible' (154). Added to that is Rodney's 'mocking' smile, which makes the likelihood of a positive outcome seem even more remote (154).

Kathy pretends 'to examine a jigsaw', which metaphorically suggests that they are going through the motions of looking for Ruth's 'possible' without true conviction or belief that it will really matter (155). Nevertheless, there is some hope the 'possible' could represent a missing part of the 'jigsaw' that could make their world and future prospects make more sense.

The L-shaped motif is repeated, as we see 'a dozen desks arranged in regular L-shaped patterns' (156). It reminds the reader that all the students are learners and that sometimes learning new things can be painful, as when Ruth finds out from Kathy that not all chess pieces move in L-shapes, earlier in the narrative.

It turns out that Ruth's 'possible' is 'around fifty' with 'dark hair' worn in 'a simple pony tail', which makes her seem similar to Ruth. Kathy admits there is 'more than a hint of Ruth' about her and in this dystopia hints seems more important than substantial evidence a lot of the time.

Ruth's reaction to to reenact her imaginary horses, as she sits on a 'damp and crumbling' wall 'like she was astride a horse' (158). Perhaps this represents the victory of imagination, albeit on a temporary basis. However, all is not well, judging by the pathetic fallacy employed by the writer. Already the elements are destroying her, with 'a breeze messing up her hair, and the bright winter' sun 'making her crinkle up her eyes' (158). There is an eerie echo to the days of donation that await students in the future with the depiction of Ruth 'grimacing in the light' (158).

The students decide to follow the 'possible', who heads 'through a door - into "The Portway Studios"' (159). This 'possible' appears to have a glamorous link to the world of music, fashion or photography, judging by the name of the establishment. Perhaps that is a bridge too far, even for an ex-Hailsham student.

Kathy loses herself in 'the sheer peacefulness' of the art studio, when the students follow the 'possible' in. Sea imagery is present, as the writer describes 'a bit of fishing net or a rotting piece from a boat' (160). The overall impression is decay. This does not bode well for the students, particularly Ruth for has the highest hopes of salvation, at this stage in the narrative.

The depressing revelation is not long in coming, as Kathy states: 'the more we heard her [the 'possible'] and looked at her, the less she seemed like Ruth' (161). It is almost as if Ruth has been punished with disappointment for seeking out out the truth.

Once again, the writer uses pathetic fallacy to show the impact. This time the students are 'hit' by the wind (162). Ruth says 'nothing', but gives 'a little shrug' after Chrissie apologises. Chrissie's apology does not appear completely genuine as she emits 'a small laugh' before saying 'sorry' (162).

Kathy and Tommy feel 'a sort of resentment' towards Chrissie and Rodney (163). Kathy appears to think that the latter pair are envious of ex-Hailsham students, for 'all kinds of possibilities' are 'open' to them (163). Therefore, there is no real equality in their relationship with students that have not been at Hailsham.

Ruth reacts to the disappointment with a discomforting revelation, stating that all the students are 'modelled from trash. Junkies, prostitutes, winos, tramps. Convicts, maybe' (164). The reader cannot help wondering why the dregs of society are used as models, if Ruth's outburst is true that 'a clone model' should be looked for 'in the gutter' (164). The reader can only guess that the down and out are so desperate for money that they allow themselves to be cloned to raise some cash.

Kathy is 'upset' by either Ruth's reaction or Chrissie and Rodney's intention to visit Martin or both (165). Ruth has little sympathy for her friend, as she states that Kathy 'never likes straight talking' (165). Tommy shows loyalty towards Kathy by saying: 'If we're splitting, then I'll stay with Kath' (165). In contrast,

Ruth is seen by the reader in a negative light, as she glares 'at him in a fury' before turning and striding off.

Chapter Fifteen

Tommy continues to be depicted as a kind character as he rationalises Ruth's behaviour as 'letting off steam' and wants to get Kathy 'a sort of present' (166).

He is so eager to please and find Kathy's lost tape, but Tommy cannot remember the exact name of the artist: he thinks it is 'Julie Bridges or something' (167). Although, he forgets the details, he shows sensitivity towards Kathy and other people's suffering. You would think that this would earmark him to be a good carer in the future.

It is interesting that the writer chooses 'Woolworth's' as the place where Tommy hopes to find the lost tape (168). The word 'worth' in the name is important, as the item is almost priceless to Kathy.

Kathy reveals that metaphorically it feels 'like every cloud' has 'blown away', as her spirits are lifted by Tommy's generous spirit (169). Through pathetic fallacy, the writer suggests they are warmer when it comes to hunting down the lost tape, when 'a dusty corner lit up by a shaft of sun' is mentioned. It is almost as if divine intervention will lend a hand to make their quest successful.

Of course, Kathy finds it and Tommy's reaction is to say: 'I wish I'd found it' (170). They both naively believe it could be the exact same copy, although Kathy realises 'there might be thousands of these knocking about' (170).

The mood begins to turn more sombre as, after Tommy buys the tape for her, the pair begin 'going up a steeply climbing path' (171). They continue despite 'the chilly wind', which suggests something less pleasant is about to come.

Tommy initiates a discussion about 'what the Gallery was for' (172). The word 'puzzle' is used again, suggesting that the pair are slowly trying to work out what is really going on in their dystopian world.

Then Tommy recalls what Madame told Roy J. about 'pictures, poetry, all that kind of stuff' revealing what the students are 'like inside' (173). It is difficult to imagine why that is important, unless the some students will be selected for brain donations. However, the implication is that if students can reveals through their art that they have a soul, then perhaps the donations can be deferred.

Continuing to try to make sense of it all, Tommy says: 'That's why Miss Lucy had to admit she's been wrong, telling me that it [creativity] didn't really matter' (174). Tommy has concluded that if you don't 'get stuff in Madame's gallery, then you were as good as throwing away that chance' of a better future away (174).

Kathy ponders what Tommy has said, revealing that: 'If Tommy's theory was right, if Madame was connected to us for the sole purpose of deferring our donations when, later on, we fell in love, then it made sense' (175). Kathy believes that would explain why Madame was so affected by seeing her 'swaying around, clutching a pillow' in the 'dorm' (175).

The pair of them believe that evidence of love and creativity may make students able to 'apply' for deferment (176). This explains why Tommy has been working on drawing 'his imaginary animals' (176). The selection process appears very competitive to the students, as they try to make sense of it all.

Tommy believes that 'there's only obvious way forward. And that's to find Madame' (177). He believes that Madame has the answers to their questions and possibly can throw some light on the application process.

There is another question, though, that he addresses to Kathy: 'Even if what Ruth says is right, and I don't think it is, why are you looking through old porn mags for your possibles?' (178). Kathy is in 'tears' and cannot really explain her actions. It shows that she is more emotional and instinctive than she sometimes appears.

Kathy attempts to explain her mixed emotions by saying that if her 'model' was someone with a high sex drive, it would 'kind of explain why' she is the way she is (179). It seems that she is ashamed of the things she has done like 'going with people like that Hughie...' (179). Using ellipsis, the writer shows us how emotional Kathy is about her sexuality.

Tommy does not judge his friend. He says: 'I don't think it's necessarily a bad thing' (180). However, he tells her 'it's stupid looking through those [pornographic] magazines' for her clone model (180). Perhaps he thinks it is futile and also depressing for Kathy to search low-lifes to find a match.

Ruth returns with Chrissie and Rodney. Ruth makes a 'fuss' of Kathy, which makes her forgive her for behaving 'badly' (181). Kathy reveals that 'it felt like the three of us were close again' as they return home 'with the darkness setting in' (181). The 'darkness' suggests that the three are closer in ignorance; the metaphorical light of the truth seems to make them part company.

Chapter Sixteen

The idea of smoke and mirrors appears again, as Kathy discusses 'the air of secrecy' that made it easier for her to conceal that Tommy has bought her the Judy Bridgewater tape (182). The longer Kathy keeps it secret, the more 'guilty' she feels (182).

Of course, Tommy has a secret of his own: 'his imaginary animals' (183). Interestingly, he shows them to Kathy in 'the goosehouse', which has a door which 'was permanently off its hinges' (183). It seems to be an unhinged place, where acts of madness take place. It suggests that Tommy is mad to think his animal drawings will change his fate.

Nevertheless, it seems Tommy has stumbled on some sort of truth, as the writer describes the place using positive pathetic fallacy: 'sunlight was pouring through the skylights' (184). Kathy has to hop over 'jaggy ground' to get there, so it shows she may have to make considerable effort literally and metaphorically to see things from Tommy's perspective (184).

The reader begins to wonder how similar to the students these imaginary creatures are. Bearing in mind the students are human clones, perhaps it is not so strange that Tommy has drawn animals that are 'busy', 'metallic' and 'vulnerable' (185). This seems to mirror how the students see themselves.

Meanwhile, Tommy questions the need for secrecy when it comes to his drawings. He tells Kathy what he's thinking: 'there's no reason why I should keep it all secret any more' (186). Kathy agrees.

Like Tommy, Kathy is full of questions. She is wondering why Ruth is reluctant to remember trivial events at Hailsham. It all comes to a head when Kathy recalls how 'the rhubarb patch was out of bounds' (187). Ruth puts on 'her puzzled look' and this irritates Kathy (187). Perhaps the rhubarb patch is part of the puzzle, which accounts for the writer's choice of words. Rhubarb could represent the donors, who are also harvested. There is the implication that they are rhubarb fools, believing everything they are told.

Similarly, the donors' body parts come to mind as Ruth peers 'at the spines' of Kathy's cassettes (188). Ruth has just discovered the Judy Bridgewater tape, although Kathy suspects that 'it hadn't been by chance at all'. Perhaps Ruth is a calculating individual. The spine motif shows how laid bare Kathy is by the discovery.

Thereafter, Kathy believes that 'the way the conversation' goes 'after that' may be 'something controlled by Ruth' (189). Kathy appears to want to avoid taking any responsibility for the fact that they begin 'laughing about his [Tommy's] animals' (189). Perhaps, Kathy does not want to appear cruel, but her actions show that she can be as insensitive as Ruth, at times.

Ruth is portrayed more sensitively, reading beneath 'a big willow', which symbolically suggests that she may about to suffer some kind of loss (190). The picture is completed by 'gravestones', linking Ruth with death (190).

However, it appears that Ruth is just as insensitive as ever as she commences teasing Tommy about his animals, smiling and shaking 'her head' (191). Tommy's response shows his increasing maturity as he says 'nothing' and continues 'with his stretching'. Tommy has stretched his personality metaphorically and he is now able to ignore the jokes at his expense rather than flying into a tantrum.

Eventually, as the teasing continues, Tommy becomes 'child-like again' (192). He looks to Kathy for help and in retrospect, she 'could have done something' (192). In front of Ruth, Kathy appears weak: she is far too malleable.

In the end, Kathy notices Tommy looking at her like she is 'a rare butterfly' (193). This simile suggests that Kathy is delicate and beautiful. She decides it's time she 'marched' off, which suggests there is something quite aggressive and militaristic about her action (193).

Chapter Seventeen

Using water imagery, which clearly relates to tearful emotions, the writer has Kathy describe the 'powerful tides tugging' her away from Ruth and Tommy (194). Like water running downhill, the students' lives have a 'natural course': to become a carer (194).

Talking about their situation becomes increasingly difficult with Tommy's 'animals or what happened in the churchyard' becoming more taboo subject that they 'never mentioned' (195). At this stage in the narrative, it seems there is very little chance of a proper reconciliation between Tommy, Kathy and Ruth, as they are afraid to speak honestly. Perhaps that is because their fear of the future is bothering them more and more.

Nevertheless, Kathy attempts to be 'conciliatory' with Ruth (196). The setting of the bus shelter with its 'cobwebs up on the rafters' does not seem to augur well for their conversation but Ruth accepts what Kathy is saying (196).

However, true to form, Ruth strikes back in a calculating manner. While she is 'picking at some moulding flakes of wood', she is choosing her time to hit back (197). Ruth reminds Kathy that Tommy 'doesn't like girls who've been with ... well, you know, with this person and that' (197). She clearly is perceptive enough to notice that Kathy harbours strong emotions for Tommy, and now Ruth has made it clear that her friend has no chance of winning his affection. Ruth's comments are designed to hurt.

Kathy comes back at her with a reminiscence that seems insignificant on the surface: James B. coming down through the rhubarb patch' (198). Ruth can't see 'what was wrong with that', which infuriates Kathy who believes her friend is being 'false' (198).

With relationships becoming tense, perhaps it's no surprise that Kathy tells Keffers that she wants 'to start her training to become a carer' (199). Kathy keeps her 'distance' from Ruth and Tommy and makes her decision alone (199). This shows a greater maturity and suggests she is ready to embrace her future.

Chapter Eighteen

Part three begins with Kathy explaining how being a carer suits her 'fine' (203). She mentions how she feels 'demoralised' when a donor 'completes' when 'no one anticipated complications' (203). She also finds it difficult to deal with 'solitude', especially after growing up 'surrounded by crowds of people' (203).

However, Kathy has adapted well to her new life and says she has 'grown to quite like' even the solitude

(204). Like the 'desk-lamps' in her bedsit, she has learned to 'bend', or be flexible (204).

Laura hasn't been so fortunate. Kathy describes her 'wearing a shapeless blue anorak' (205). It seems that the colour blue may indicate a miserable state of mind, as seems the case earlier in the novel when Tommy blows his top in his 'light blue polo shirt' (8).

From Laura's recollection of rumours, we find out that Ruth has 'had a really bad first donation' (206). Additionally, Laura suggests that Kathy 'become Ruth's carer' (206). On the surface, it sounds like a difficult task, as Ruth and Kathy 'weren't such great friends by the end' of their time together in the Cottages (206).

Before Laura leaves, she talks to Kathy about the closure of Hailsham. Kathy reveals that the topic brings them 'close again' (207). They hug 'spontaneously', overwhelmed by emotions (207). Perhaps both are perturbed about how they will be viewed now that they are ex-students of a defunct rather than a respected institution.

We are subtly reminded that Kathy and her friends are clones when the image of 'balloons' with 'faces and shaped ears' is depicted by the writer (208). Like the balloons full of 'helium', the clones are full of hot air. The balloons look 'like a little tribe, bobbing in the air above their owner, waiting for him' (208). Likewise, the clones are powerless awaiting death by donation.

Kathy's sensitivity is exemplified by her 'worrying that one of the strings would come unravelled and a single balloon would sail off up into the cloudy sky' (209). It seems that Kathy holds great store in togetherness and yet she leads a solitary life as a carer. Nevertheless, she still has her memories of Hailsham that make her feel part of something greater.

When Kathy meets Ruth again, their conversation is 'guarded' (210). Once again, they have 'to pretend' that certain things had not 'happened' (210). It does not seem as if they will be able to get over their differences.

Just when Kathy is about to give up the idea of being Ruth's carer, the rescue of their relationship is achieved through 'the boat' (211). Once again, the writer uses water imagery to show the characters rising above difficulties or, in other words, floating like a boat.

It transpires that the 'old fishing boat' that Ruth is talking about has 'a little cabin for a couple of fishermen to squeeze into when it's stormy' (212). It is reassuring for them to think about a place that provides shelter from storms.

It turns out that Tommy is staying nearby the boat. Eventually, Kathy is convinced that 'unless' they hear 'from Tommy telling' them 'not to', they would 'show up at the Kingsfield on a particular afternoon the following week (213).

Chapter Nineteen

One of the aspects of Kingsfield that troubles Kathy is the 'traffic' noise (214). She mentions that there is 'no real sense of peace and quiet' (214). In many way, it is a daunting prospect to visit Tommy there.

The place seems to resemble something from the war with its 'white bunker-like two-storey buildings' (215). When Kathy sees Tommy, she notes that he appears 'about a stone heavier' (215). We can only assume that donating has affected his mobility, and his 'faded green track-suit top' suggests that he misses his days of sporting prowess.

The writer uses the sense of smell to convey the idea that Tommy the donor is a very different proposition to Tommy the student. Kathy reveals she 'could smell a faint odour of something medical on him' (216). Even she cannot 'identify' it, so it suggests he has donated an unusual organ as Kathy, accustomed though she is to donors, has not come across the smell before (216).

Notwithstanding the odour, Kathy still feels 'close' to Tommy, particularly when he makes a 'sudden laughing noise' which shuts Ruth up (217). It seems that Kathy's rivalry with Ruth over Tommy's affections is still intact, although being a carer, Kathy appears to have the upper hand now.

Kathy parks the car by 'a clump of sycamores', which may symbolise that Tommy and Ruth are on the threshold of life and death (218). Kathy says that the two donors are 'waiting almost like children' (218). Their physical condition has made them more compliant and ready obey instructions. They've become less active and consequently have become more passive. Kathy has to help Ruth 'to pass through' a fence and even Tommy has 'a hint of a limp' (218).

In Ruth's case, her 'frail' condition has affected her 'confidence' (218, 219). Using animal imagery, the writer describes Tommy as 'looking sheepish' (219). He perhaps cannot completely understand the complexity of the world he lives in, but he has a strong emotional instinct that makes him sensitive to others' feelings.

Like donors after donations, the writer describes the woods with 'ghostly dead trunks poking out of the soil' (220). Even the escape from the inevitable future represented by the boat looks bleak 'sitting beached in the marshes under the weak sun' (220). However, Ruth describes the scene as 'beautiful' (220). It seems that the characters are ready to settle for less, as even Kathy seems proud of her bedsit. Like the donors, the boat is fading away with its paint 'cracking' (220).

The discussion moves to the prospect of completing during a 'second donation', as that is what rumours suggest happened to Chrissie (221). Kathy informs Ruth and Tommy that there is 'no big conspiracy' (221). She tells them 'it happens' sometimes, but it's uncommon (221). The conventional Kathy is an effective mouthpiece for the system.

The argument brings Ruth back to life, as 'the flash of anger' is much more like her (222). She tries to use the fact that Kathy is a carer to get Tommy on her side of the argument.

However, Tommy is absorbed in his own thoughts about why he became a donor so quickly. He puts it down to his inability to learn 'to drive' (223). By contrast, he declares himself 'a pretty good donor'

(223). Ruth thinks she is similar in that respect. The pair have taken to donating as if it is a vocation that they can be proud of. Ruth gives the act a sense of duty by saying: 'it's what we're supposed to be doing' (223).

Ruth continues to have a superior attitude, criticising a poster they were 'passing' (224). Once again, Tommy and Kathy gang up on Ruth, disagreeing with her.

Kathy reduces Ruth to a 'whisper' as she stops by a poster of an open-plan office, with 'smart smiling people' (225). Ruth is reluctant to 'remember' the disappointment. Perhaps Kathy is sadistically enjoying dominating her old friend, who used to be the dominant one before becoming a donor.

Kathy and Tommy continue to hound Ruth about the attempt to find her clone model and what she should have done about it. Ruth's reply is: 'How could I have looked into it?' (226). Of course, the other two, for all their criticism, only have questions rather than answers.

However, Kathy blurts out that Ruth 'should have gone to Madame and asked' (226). Kathy views this outburst as a 'mistake' that results in Ruth's moment of 'triumph' (227). This exchange shows us that Kathy still sees herself in competition with Ruth.

The conversation becomes confessional for Ruth, who admits she 'kept' Kathy 'and Tommy apart' (228). She seems to feel guilty about that as she describes it as 'the worst thing' she did.

Ruth wants to recompense Tommy and Kathy for lost time, so she hands him 'a crumpled piece of paper' with Madame's address on it (229). Kathy sobs and cannot, at this stage of the narrative, think of applying for a deferral with Tommy as her lover.

After dropping Tommy off, Kathy observes that 'all the guardedness' between her and Ruth 'evaporated' (230). It seems as if the competition has now run its course, with Ruth getting ever nearer to completion.

Then Kathy reports the complications following Ruth's 'second donation' (231). There are doubt that she will make it, but Kathy imagines Ruth seeing 'inside herself, so she could patrol and marshal all the better the separate areas of pain in her body' (231). Even in this terrible state, Kathy sees Ruth in a commanding position.

On Ruth's deathbed, Kathy admits that she's 'going to become Tommy's carer' as soon as she can (232). She hopes her friend heard her before passing away.

Chapter Twenty

The writer uses the recurring 'L-shaped' motif to describe Tommy's room at the Kingsfield (232). This could show that he is still on a steep learning curve, especially as he even has 'a little school desk' in the room (232). There is something quite childish and innocent about the description, like Kathy reading traditional adventure stories like The Odyssey and One Thousand and One Nights to him.

Although they begin to have a sex life, Kathy is aware that being a donor made it difficult for Tommy at first. As 'he was still recovering [...] it wasn't the first thing on his mind' (234).

Their relationship seems enhanced by 'the way the sun came in through the frosted glass so [...] that it felt like autumn light' (235). Already waiting for his third donation, it seems as if the light reminds Kathy how precious their time together is.

Tommy decides to show Kathy 'sketches of a kind of frog - except with a long tail as though part of it had stayed a tadpole' (236). Perhaps Tommy sees himself as not fully grown yet, like the frog he has drawn.

Kathy still has a feeling they 'were down all of this too late' (237). She is also worried that Tommy's drawings look 'laboured' (237). It's like he has tried too hard, 'almost like they'd been copied' (237).

The writer reveals through pathetic fallacy their future prospects as a pair are poor, with the rain 'bucketing down' (238). Additionally, 'Tommy's room was almost dark' (238).

However, Kathy reveals that she has seen Madame in Littlehampton. Using water imagery, the writer mentions houses called 'Wavecrest' and 'Seaview' to show what a monumentally emotional moment it is for the two of them (239).

Now that they actually have a chance of asking Madame for a deferral, the whole plan is 'definitely a bit scary' (240). They agree to take up to 'twenty' of Tommy's imaginary animals with them to make a stronger case for deferral.

Chapter Twenty One

They park 'the car behind the bingo hall', which suggests they are hoping for luck on the quest for referral (241). Tommy is feeling 'woozy' after re-doing some of his medical tests, so the day does not start well (241).

The 'setting sun' seems to suggest their mission will end in failure as they follow Madame. Even the reassuring 'water itself' is invisible, as their hopes seem to fade with the sunset (242).

When they finally confront Madame in this climactic scene, her eyes are 'cold' (243). Madame seems more like an adversary than an ally. She looks at them like they are 'a pair of spiders [...] set to crawl towards her (243).

They are invited into Madame's house, where they can 'smell the old furniture, which was probably Victorian' like the literature Kathy and Ruth have studied (244). The theme of education comes to the fore with the description of 'a picture, woven like a tapestry, of a strange owl-like bird' (244). As well as suggesting wisdom, the owl conveys the idea that the teacher observes everything, which must be quite disconcerting for Kathy and Tommy.

After disappearing briefly, Madame confronts the pair, 'staring' at them. Kathy tried 'to see past her, but it' is 'just darkness' (245). It seems increasingly unlikely that this visit will end productively for them.

Madame discourages physical contact tucking 'her shoulders in tightly as she' passes 'between them'

(246). Her position 'in front of the heavy velvet curtains' makes it seem as Madame is putting on some kind of performance (246).

Madame does appear to have a sentimental side as she has 'little tears in her eyes' as she questions the validity of Kathy and Tommy's love (247). She really wants to know why they have come to her, though.

After talking about her collection of students' art, Madame seems a little unnatural when she says: 'Do I go too far?' (248). She is hardly welcoming to the pair, as Kathy is left with the distinct feeling that she has 'something' disgusting on her sleeve (248).

Kathy soon realises there is 'someone listening behind' them 'in the darkened half of the room' (249). She realises Madame's questions are for that listener. The writer is carefully building tension by revealing the full situation bit by bit.

Sound imagery follows as Kathy hears 'a sound, a mechanical one' (250). Then 'a shape' moves towards them (250). It turns out to be a wheelchair-bound Miss Emily, who may be awaiting donations to prolong her life. Miss Emily is described as 'frail' and 'contorted' (250). Only her voice is recognisable. We are left with the image of Madame's 'eyes blazing' as the writer ends the chapter on another cliff-hanger with the reader wanting to know what will happen next.

Chapter Twenty Two

Miss Emily has some kind words for both Tommy and Kathy, remembering his 'big heart' (251). Ironically, that same organ may be cut out for a donation.

Compared to Madame (Marie-Claude), Miss Emily seems more sympathetic on the surface when she reveals that Madame's view of the students' deferral rumour is: 'If they're so foolish, let them believe it' (252).

Kathy and Tommy find out that deferrals have always been 'a little fantasy' (253). Miss Emily also informs them that Hailsham was set up as a 'more humane and better way' of setting up clones for donation (253).

'The Morningdale scandal' is mentioned a number of times by Miss Emily, as if it was a watershed and ended up a reason for Hailsham's closure (254). It just adds another question to the narrative, not answered straight away and leaving the reader guessing along with the main characters.

Finally, Miss Emily reveals that the Gallery was indeed set up to 'prove' that the students 'had souls' (255). It seems that until Hailsham it was generally doubted that clones could have them 'at all' (255).

Before Hailsham clones 'existed only to supply medical science', according to Miss Emily (256). The school used the art to prove that the children were 'fully human' (256).

The history lesson continues, with Miss Emily explaining how 'in the early fifties' science moved so 'rapidly' (257). People wanted to be cured and it suited them to believe 'organs appeared from nowhere' (257).

Miss Emily admits the students 'were kept in the shadows' (258). It is almost as if they are like Victor Frankenstein's monster. That fear came to a head when James Morningdale wanted to produce children with 'superior intelligence' and 'superior athleticism' (258). Like Frankenstein, he carries out his work in a remote part of Scotland.

Water imagery is used again by the writer, this time to show how society reacted emotionally to the idea of clones. Miss Emily mentions an 'awful television series' (259). She says that 'contributed to the turning of the ride' (259).

Madame seems quite bitter after Miss Emily completes her lecture, saying: 'Don't try and ask them to thank you' (260). The main characters appear to be stunned.

Miss Emily explains further that the students were 'lucky pawns' at Hailsham. Of course, in chess, pawns are often sacrificed for the greater good, just like the donors.

Additionally, Miss Emily reveals that Miss Lucy's services were dispensed with because she was 'too theoretical' (262). Miss Lucy believed that students should 'be made more aware' (262). Perhaps, these ideas were too revolutionary for Hailsham.

The whole principle behind Hailsham was 'sheltering' the students (263). The truth could have demotivated the future donors.

However, Miss Emily is ready to admit the 'revulsion' she felt for the students at Hailsham (264). Nevertheless, she claims she 'fought those feelings' and 'won' (264). She seems immensely proud of what she achieved, no matter what the cost.

With Miss Emily being driven off, Madame remains for some parting words in 'the fading light' (265). She keeps calling Kathy 'a mind-reader' and the reader begins to wonder if the clones really do have superpowers. Perhaps that's why they have to be used for donations.

Madame begins to reveal why she was so touched by spotting Kathy dancing by herself with 'eyes closed', holding a pillow, full of 'yearning' (266). This seems to put to bed the idea that Kathy is a mind-reader, for she guessed what Madame was thinking incorrectly. Instead, Madame was thinking that Kathy's pillow represented 'the old kind world' (267).

After they leave the house, Tommy's reaction is reminiscent of Frankenstein's monster as he heads off 'into the blackness' and begins to 'scream' (268). The almost 'full' moon makes the scene seem even more gothic as Kathy chases him into the mud (269).

Now Kathy believes that Tommy instinctively 'always knew' that their fate was completely out of their hands (270). That would explain his temper tantrums of yesteryear.

Chapter Twenty Three

The final chapter begins with Tommy becoming 'cagey' about drawing his 'animal pictures' in front of Kathy (271). The word 'cagey' indicates that he is like a domestic animal leading a life predetermined by his owners.

Kathy refers to 'a little prickle' of 'resentment' growing in Tommy towards her (272). Increasingly, he is sensing that she cannot understand what it feels like to be a donor.

The tension increases 'about a week after the notice' comes 'for his fourth donation' (273). As mentioned before, that usually indicates death. Tommy tells Kathy that it's the lack of certainty that makes the fourth donation worse.

The questions are haunting Tommy, who is wondering if 'after the fourth donation, even if you've technically completed, you're still conscious' (274). Tommy imagines surviving on a life support machine with his remaining organs slowly being stripped away.

Finally, Tommy reveals that he thinks he 'ought to get a different carer' (275). Although Kathy is expecting him to say this, she still feels 'angry' (275). Tommy explains that he feels embarrassed by his recent 'kidney trouble' and expects worse to follow (275).

Once again, Tommy mentions that Kathy doesn't understand because she's 'not a donor' (276). She walks off in disgust as he mentions that 'Ruth would have understood' (276). Her old rivalry with Ruth still hasn't died.

Tommy talks about how he thinks 'about this river somewhere, with the water moving really fast' (277). In the end, 'the current's too strong' for the couple in the water to stay together (277). The touching moment is made all the more memorable by the use of water imagery, making the reader think of tears.

The next significant moment is when Kathy arrives in Tommy's room 'on a crisp December afternoon' when she asks him if he is 'glad' that Ruth died before 'finding out everything' (278). Tommy thinks it was best for Ruth not to know as 'she always wanted to believe in things' (279).

Before heading off for his fourth donation, Tommy reveals to Ruth how he imagined he 'was splashing through water' when he scored a goal while playing football (280). He explains how good it felt. As well as emphasising the emotional tension, the water here represents how Tommy has remained playful until the better end.

Now Kathy is left with 'memories of Tommy and of Ruth' and no less importantly Hailsham (281). She admits after Tommy's death she drove to Norfolk, possibly because she 'felt like looking at all those flat fields of nothing and the huge grey skies' (281). It appears to be a less-than-comforting view, a bit like her own future.

The reader is left with images of 'all sorts of rubbish' collecting along a 'fence' (282). The 'debris' emphasises the shabby way donors have been treated (282). Meanwhile, the fence symbolises the line that clones cannot cross and how it prevents them taking their place in wider society.

Essay writing tips

<u>Use a variety of connectives</u>

Have a look of this list of connectives. Which of these would you choose to use?

'ADDING' DISCOURSE MARKERS

- AND

- ALSO

- AS WELL AS

- MOREOVER

- TOO

- FURTHERMORE

- ADDITIONALLY

I hope you chose 'additionally', 'furthermore' and 'moreover'. Don't be afraid to use the lesser discourse markers, as they are also useful. Just avoid using those ones over and over again. I've seen essays from Key

Stage 4 students that use the same discourse marker for the opening sentence of each paragraph! Needless to say, those essays didn't get great marks!

Okay, here are some more connectives for you to look at. Select the best ones.

'SEQUENCING' DISCOURSE MARKERS

- NEXT
- FIRSTLY
- SECONDLY
- THIRDLY
- FINALLY
- MEANWHILE
- AFTER
- THEN
- SUBSEQUENTLY

This time, I hope you chose 'subsequently' and 'meanwhile'.

Here are some more connectives for you to 'grade'!

'ILLUSTRATING / EXEMPLIFYING' DISCOURSE MARKERS

- FOR EXAMPLE
- SUCH AS

- FOR INSTANCE

- IN THE CASE OF

- AS REVEALED BY

- ILLUSTRATED BY

I'd probably go for 'illustrated by' or even 'as exemplified by' (which is not in the list!). Please feel free to add your own examples to the lists. Strong connectives impress examiners. Don't forget it! That's why I want you to look at some more.

'CAUSE & EFFECT' DISCOURSE MARKERS

- BECAUSE

- SO

- THEREFORE

- THUS

- CONSEQUENTLY

- HENCE

I'm going for 'consequently' this time. How about you? What about the next batch?

'COMPARING' DISCOURSE MARKERS

- SIMILARLY

- LIKEWISE

- AS WITH

- LIKE

- EQUALLY

- IN THE SAME WAY

I'd choose 'similarly' this time. Still some more to go.

'QUALIFYING' DISCOURSE MARKERS

- BUT

- HOWEVER

- WHILE

- ALTHOUGH

- UNLESS

- EXCEPT

- APART FROM

- AS LONG AS

It's 'however' for me!

'CONTRASTING' DISCOURSE MARKERS

- WHEREAS

- INSTEAD OF

- ALTERNATIVELY

- OTHERWISE

- UNLIKE

- ON THE OTHER HAND

- CONVERSELY

I'll take 'conversely' or 'alternatively' this time.

'EMPHASISING' DISCOURSE MARKERS

- ABOVE ALL

- IN PARTICULAR

- ESPECIALLY

- SIGNIFICANTLY

- INDEED

- NOTABLY

You can breathe a sigh of relief now! It's over! No more connectives. However, now I want to put our new found skills to use in our essays.

Useful information/Glossary

Allegory: extended metaphor, like the grim reaper representing death, e.g. Scrooge symbolizing capitalism.

Alliteration: same consonant sound repeating, e.g. 'She sells sea shells'.

Allusion: reference to another text/person/place/event.

Ascending tricolon: sentence with three parts, each increasing in power, e.g. 'ringing, drumming, shouting'.

Aside: character speaking so some characters cannot hear what is being said. Sometimes, an aside is directly to the audience. It's a dramatic technique which reveals the character's inner thoughts and feelings.

Assonance: same vowel sounds repeating, e.g. 'Oh no, won't Joe go?'

Bathos: abrupt change from sublime to ridiculous for humorous effect.

Blank verse: lines of unrhymed iambic pentameter.

Compressed time: when the narrative is fast-forwarding through the action.

Descending tricolon: sentence with three parts, each decreasing in power, e.g. 'shouting, talking, whispering'.

Denouement: tying up loose ends, the resolution.

Diction: choice of words or vocabulary.

Didactic: used to describe literature designed to inform, instruct or pass on a moral message.

Dilated time: opposite compressed time, here the narrative is in slow motion.

Direct address: second person narrative, predominantly using the personal pronoun 'you'.

Dramatic action verb: manifests itself in physical action, e.g. I punched him in the face.

Dramatic irony: audience knows something that the character is unaware of.

Ellipsis: leaving out part of the story and allowing the reader to fill in the narrative gap.

End-stopped lines: poetic lines that end with punctuation.

Epistolary: letter or correspondence-driven narrative.

Flashback/Analepsis: going back in time to the past, interrupting the chronological sequence.

Flashforward/Prolepsis: going forward in time to the future, interrupting the chronological sequence.

Foreshadowing/Adumbrating: suggestion of plot developments that will occur later in the narrative.

Gothic: another strand of Romanticism, typically with a wild setting, a sensitive heroine, an older man with a 'piercing gaze', discontinuous structure, doppelgangers, guilt and the 'unspeakable' (according to Eve Kosofsky Sedgwick).

Hamartia: character flaw, leading to that character's downfall.

Hyperbole: exaggeration for effect.

Iambic pentameter: a line of ten syllables beginning with a lighter stress alternating with a heavier stress in its perfect form, which sounds like a heartbeat. The stress falls on the even syllables, numbers: 2, 4, 6, 8 and 10, e.g. 'When now I think you can behold such sights'.

Intertextuality: links to other literary texts.

Irony: amusing or cruel reversal of expected outcome or words meaning the opposite to their literal meaning.

Metafiction/Romantic irony: self-conscious exposure of the devices used to create 'the truth' within a work of fiction.

Motif: recurring image use of language or idea that connects the narrative together and creates a theme or mood, e.g. 'green light' in *The Great Gatsby*.

Oxymoron: contradictory terms combined, e.g. deafening silence.

Pastiche: imitation of another's work.

Pathetic fallacy: a form of personification whereby inanimate objects show human attributes, e.g. 'the sea smiled benignly'. The originator of the term, John Ruskin in 1856, used 'the cruel, crawling foam', from Kingsley's *The Sands of Dee*, as an example to clarify what he meant by the 'morbid' nature of pathetic fallacy.

Personification: concrete or abstract object made human, often simply achieved by using a capital letter or a personal pronoun, e.g. 'Nature', or describing a ship as 'she'.

Pun/Double entendre: a word with a double meaning, usually employed in witty wordplay but not always.

Retrospective: account of events after they have occurred.

Romanticism: genre celebrating the power of imagination, spriritualism and nature.

Semantic/lexical field: related words about a single concept, e.g. king, queen and prince are all concerned with royalty.

Soliloquy: character thinks aloud, but is not heard by other characters (unlike in a monologue) giving the audience access to inner thoughts and feelings.

Style: choice of language, form and structure, and effects produced.

Synecdoche: one part of something referring to the whole, e.g. Carker's teeth represent him in *Dombey and Son*.

Syntax: the way words and sentences are placed together.

Tetracolon climax: sentence with four parts, culminating with the last part, e.g. 'I have nothing to offer but blood, toil, tears, and sweat ' (Winston Churchill).

ABOUT THE AUTHOR

Joe Broadfoot is a secondary school teacher of English and a soccer journalist, who also writes fiction and literary criticism. His former experiences as a DJ took him to far-flung places such as Tokyo, Kobe, Beijing, Hong Kong, Jakarta, Cairo, Dubai, Cannes, Oslo, Bergen and Bodo. He is now PGCE and CELTA-qualified with QTS, a first-class honours degree in Literature and an MA in Victorian Studies (majoring in Charles Dickens). Drama is close to his heart as he acted in 'Macbeth' and 'A Midsummer Night's Dream' at the Royal Northern College of Music in Manchester. More recently, he has been teaching 'Much Ado About Nothing' to 'A' Level students at a secondary school in Buckinghamshire, 'An Inspector Calls' at a school in west London 'Heroes' at a school in Kent and 'A Christmas Carol' at a school in south London.

18924692R00058

Printed in Poland
by Amazon Fulfillment
Poland Sp. z o.o., Wrocław